I AM GRATEFUL TO GOD FOR EVERYTHING! AND I BELIEVE THAT THE MEANING OF LIFE IS TO GIVE MEANING TO OTHER LIVES.
THANK YOU VERY MUCH FOR CHOOSING THIS BOOK, MAY IT BRING YOU PLEASANT AND MEMORABLE MOMENTS.

DOUGLAS TOMÉ

2023

This Book Belongs to:

____

Test Color Page

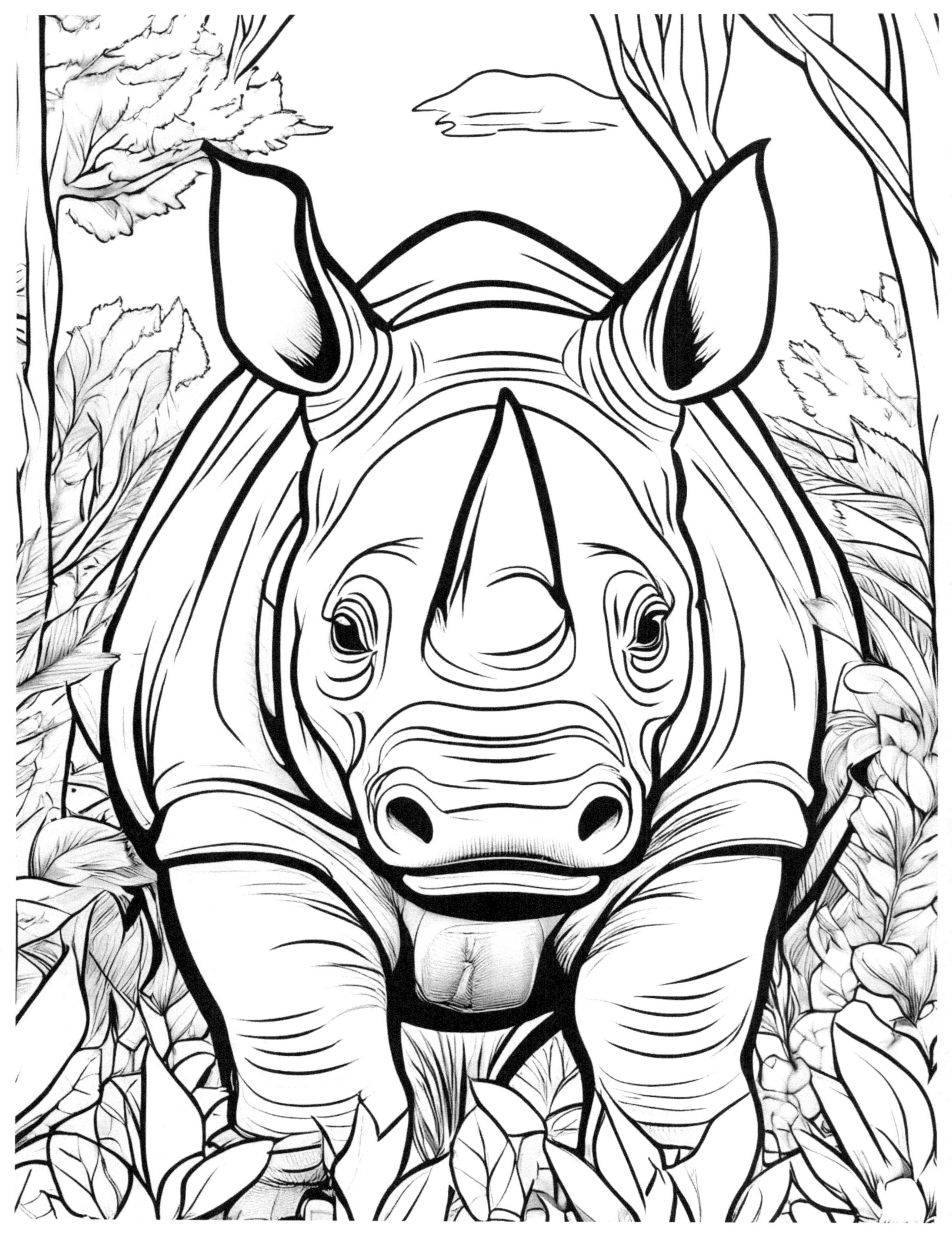